Kids
Can
Code

Understanding Coding with
LEGO
MINDSTORMS™

Patricia Harris

PowerKiDS press™

New York

Published in 2016 by The Rosen Publishing Group, Inc.
29 East 21st Street, New York, NY 10010

First Edition

Editor: Greg Roza
Book Design: Michael J. Flynn

Photo Credits: Cover (boy) Ruslan Guzov/Shutterstock.com; cover (LEGO mindstorm) zilupe/www.flickr.com/photos/zilupe/3020110950/CC BY 2.0; cover, pp. 1, 3–24 (coding background) Lukas Rs/Shutterstock.com; p. 5 wiredforlego/www.flickr.com/photos/wiredforsound23/8474697493/CC BY-NC 2.0; pp. 7, 10–22 (LEGO graphics and screenshots) the LEGO Group; p. 9 mbeo/www.flickr.com/photos/mbeo52/19526151160/CC BY-NC-ND 2.0; p. 15 Priit Tammets/www.flickr.com/photos/tammets/11463577864/CC BY 2.0; p. 17 (girl) wavebreakmedia/Shutterstock.com; p. 19 Iwan Gabovitch/www.flickr.com/photos/qubodup/16843730563/CC BY 2.0.

The LEGO name and products, including MINDSTORMS and WeDo, are trademarks of the LEGO Group, and their use in this book does not imply a recommendation or endorsement of this title by the LEGO Group.

Cataloging-in-Publication Data

Names: Patricia Harris.
Title: Understanding coding with LEGO Mindstorms™ / Patricia Harris.
Description: New York : PowerKids Press, 2016. | Series: Kids can code | Includes index.
Identifiers: ISBN 9781508144625 (pbk.) | ISBN 9781508144632 (6 pack) | ISBN 9781508144649 (library bound)
Subjects: LCSH: LEGO Mindstorms toys–Juvenile literature. | Robotics–Juvenile literature. | Robots–Design and construction–Juvenile literature.
Classification: LCC TJ211.2 H37 2016 | DDC 629.8′92–dc23

Manufactured in the United States of America

CPSIA Compliance Information: Batch #BW16PK: For Further Information contact Rosen Publishing, New York, New York at 1-800-237-9932

Contents

Playing with Code

The LEGO Group has been manufacturing its **iconic** blocks since 1958. The blocks have long been wildly popular with children and adults alike, even today when computers, video-game consoles, and electronic devices have become the most popular toys around. Long known for adapting to changing interests, the LEGO Group released the first Mindstorms kit in 1998. This was shortly after personal computers and the Internet became popular with the public. Mindstorms provides young scientists and **engineers** with the tools to explore robotics and computer programming.

Many people know how much fun it is to build with LEGO blocks. Can you imagine programming your LEGO creations to move, talk, and interact with the real world? You might be surprised to learn how easy and fun coding can be with Mindstorms.

Breaking the Code

"LEGO" is short for *leg godt*, which means "play well" in Danish. The company still lives by that motto. By creating Mindstorms—and its little sibling WeDo—LEGO has helped make computer programming fun and educational. It also teaches robotic basics. This shows that coding isn't just for scientists and computer hackers. It's something anyone can play with and enjoy.

The first Mindstorms robot most people build is Tracker. It's the easiest to build and program.

How Does It Work?

The Mindstorms box includes LEGO blocks, gears, motors, sensors, wires, and the other physical parts needed to build a robot. The picture on page 7 shows the various motors and sensors in the Mindstorms EV3 kit.

The EV3 brick is important. It follows the directions you give it and controls the other parts of the robot. The EV3 brick needs batteries as a power source, but it shares information with your computer through a **USB connection**. This is how the coded instructions you create on your computer get to the EV3 brick. When you have a program you like, you can send the entire code to the EV3 brick. Then you can run your program without the USB connection to your computer.

Breaking the Code

Mindstorms creations use sensors to interact with the real world. Sensors pick up information and send it to the EV3 brick. The brick then uses the information to make decisions based on the instructions you gave it. The touch sensor sends a signal to the EV3 brick when your robot touches an object. The color sensor recognizes color, and the **infrared** sensor detects objects in front of it. These sensors work together to tell your robot when to stop, turn, back up, and many other reactions.

Overview

Large Motor
+ Lets you program
precise and powerful
robotic action.

EV3 Brick
+ Serves as the control center
and power station for your
robot.

Touch Sensor
+ Recognizes three
conditions: touched,
bumped, and released.

Color Sensor
+ Recognizes seven different
colors and measures light
intensity.

Remote Infrared Beacon
+ Remote controls your robot
from a distance.

Medium Motor
+ Maintains precision, while
trading some power for
compact size and faster
response.

Infrared Sensor
+ Detects objects and can
track and find the Remote
Infrared Beacon.

Basic Rules of Coding

The Mindstorms kit comes with the **hardware** you need to make robots, but you need to download the Mindstorms **software** from LEGO.com. However, before you can begin to learn about coding in any language, Mindstorms included, you need to know the following important rules.

Rule 1: Coders must know what they want the computer to do and write a plan.

Rule 2: Coders must use special words to have the computer take input, make choices, and take action.

Rule 3: Coders need to think about what tasks can be put into a group.

Rule 4: Coders need to use **logic** with AND, OR, NOT, and other logic statements as key words.

Rule 5: Coders must explore the **environment** and understand how it works.

Want to make this robot move?
Then you must follow the five
rules of coding!

9

Let's Get Started

At the opening screen for Mindstorms, click the Plus tab to go into a new programming environment. If you click on a robot, you'll see a drop-down box with the directions for making that robot.

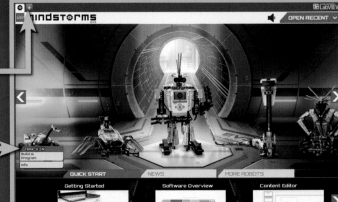

tab to go to a new program

drop-down box that lets you build the Tracker

To start learning about coding with Mindstorms, let's use Tracker built up to step 12. That will give us a very simple robot to experiment with. Notice the wires and **ports** that allow the brick to communicate with the motors.

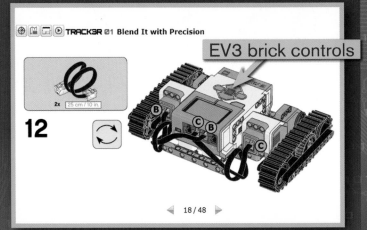

EV3 brick controls

Shown here is a simple example of Mindstorms code. Notice that the pieces "snap together" somewhat like LEGO blocks! The green block is the motor steering block. This code tells the EV3 brick to turn on the motors connected to ports B and C so the robot can go forward.

Each part of this code helps control how Tracker will move. The direction is set to 0, or straight ahead. The power tells Tracker how fast to move. Revolutions tells the motors how many times to turn the wheels.

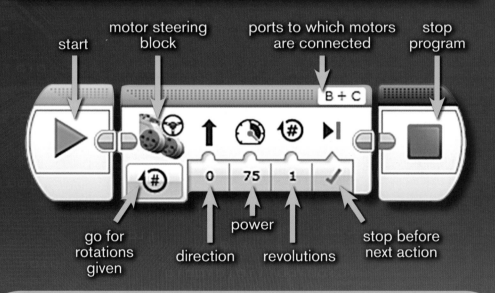

start | motor steering block | ports to which motors are connected | stop program

go for rotations given | direction | power | revolutions | stop before next action

Breaking the Code

The EV3 brick is very easy to operate. Turn the unit on with the center button and wait for a start menu and a green light. Press the right arrow two times until the group of squares is chosen. Then press the down button three times so Brick Program is chosen. To shut down the robot, press the button on the top right of the EV3 brick.

Understanding the Environment

The environment for the Mindstorms coding language is a **graphical** user **interface**, or GUI (GOO-ee). This is different from many traditional coding languages because it uses graphics instead of words to create a program.

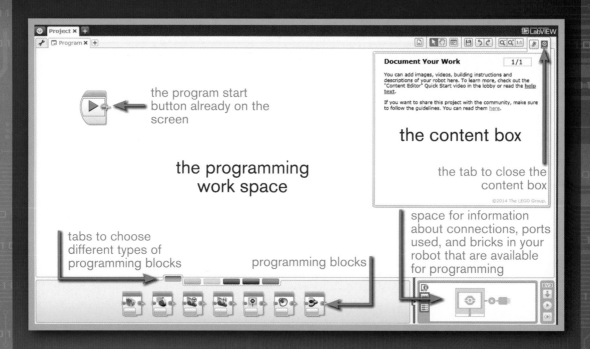

the program start button already on the screen

the programming work space

Document Your Work 1/1

You can add images, videos, building instructions and descriptions of your robot here. To learn more, check out the "Content Editor" Quick Start video in the lobby or read the help text.

If you want to share this project with the community, make sure to follow the guidelines. You can read them here.

the content box

the tab to close the content box

©2014 The LEGO Group.

space for information about connections, ports used, and bricks in your robot that are available for programming

tabs to choose different types of programming blocks

programming blocks

Plan: a simple program to go forward and back

The next block is go forward 10 revolutions

B + C

Programming with Mindstorms is simple. Look at the programming blocks along the bottom of the screen. Coders drag and drop these blocks into the workspace. The more blocks a coder drags there, the longer and more complex the code gets. The motor steering block is just one kind of programming block. The code below uses blue comment blocks to give a short plan and to tell what each block of code does. It also has start and stop blocks. All the blocks fit together like LEGO blocks.

You can also use the content box to record information about your program. However, comment blocks allow you to include notes right in the code itself. The comment blocks don't affect the program.

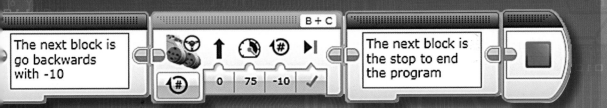

The next block is go backwards with -10

B + C

0   75   -10

The next block is the stop to end the program

Working with Wires

Connecting wires allow you to link your comments to the code so they aren't directly in the line of code. Move your cursor over a connecting point on a block of code until you see a spool of wire. Then click on the spool and drag the wire to another block to link them.

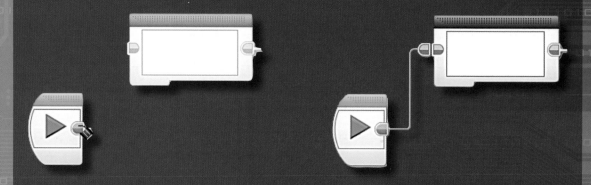

Wires are also important when you want two things to happen at the same time. You can connect a wire from the start block to a sound block and one to a movement block. Then when you start the program, the robot will move forward and play the sound at the same time. You need to add a stop to one of the blocks so your robot will turn off when it completes the actions.

Here's the code that allows the robot to move and play a sound at the same time. Look at the icons and numbers of these control blocks. Can you figure out how they affect the robot's actions?

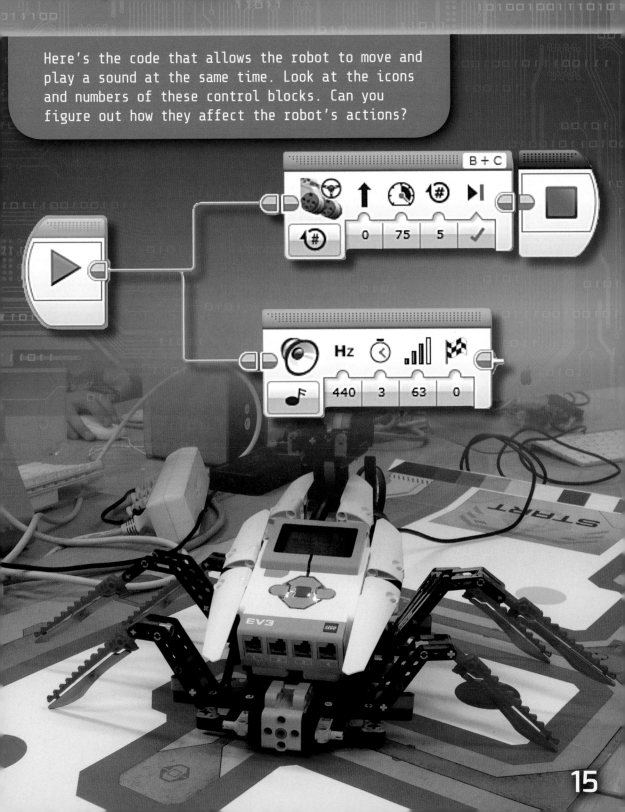

B + C

0   75   5   ✓

Hz   440   3   63   0

EV3

Loop-the-Loop!

This picture shows another program that performs two actions at the same time. It builds on the code from the previous page. Be careful when you try this one! The "-5" in the steering block means the robot goes backward.

The orange block with "01" at the top is a loop or repeat block. The loop block goes around one or more other blocks and makes them repeat. This loop has a sound block that plays for 0.5 second followed by a block that says wait for 0.5 second. These two blocks work together to make a beeping sound. The **infinity** symbol (∞) under the two arrows in the loop means the sound will go on until the program stops. It's a good thing there's a stop block at the end of the steering block!

loop block

infinity symbol

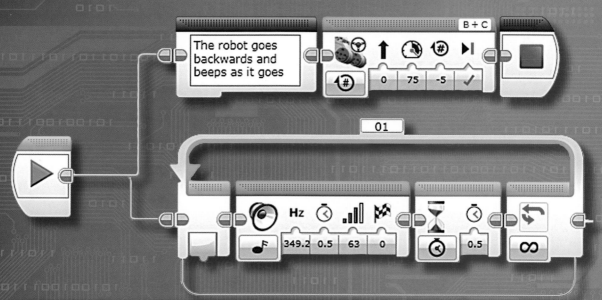

Programmers often reuse sections of code, rather than typing them over and over again. This is smart coding. The loop block gives you an idea of how this works.

Time to Turn

Now that we know how to get Tracker moving, let's create a loop code to make it drive in a square. To move the robot forward, the revolutions must be set for a positive number. A time block tells the robot to pause for a second, and the line of code is done.

Driving in a square requires Tracker to make **90-degree** turns. To write the code for a turn, you need a large motor block. This block tells the EV3 brick to move just one of Tracker's treads (B in this example), which causes the robot to **pivot** 90 degrees. The revolutions in this example are set for 3.1, but you'll need to experiment to find the best number for your code.

large motor block

The first code shows forward movement and a pause. The second code shows the turn and wait. Use start and stop blocks to test these small lines of code before moving on.

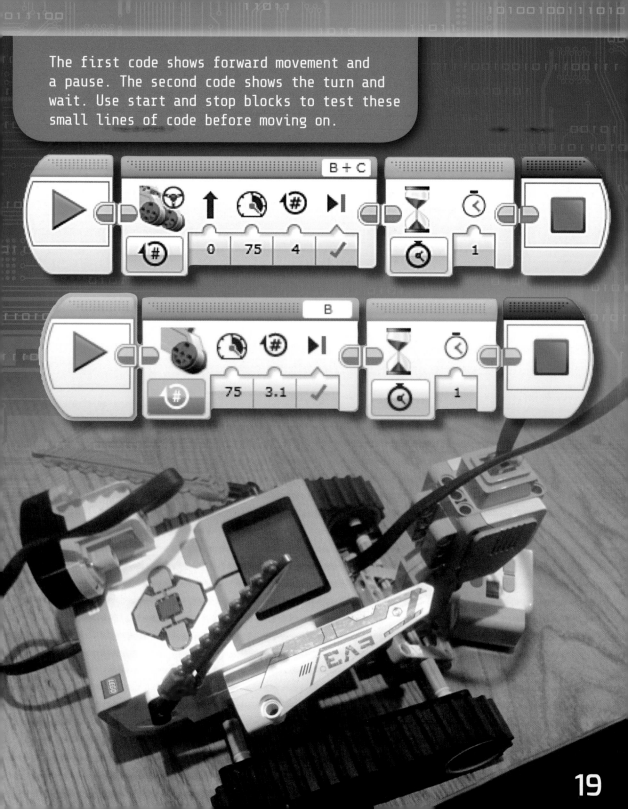

B + C

0 75 4 ✓

1

B

75 3.1 ✓

1

At this point, the code makes Tracker drive in a straight line, rest 1 second, turn 90 degrees and rest again. When the pieces of code work the way you want them to, you can make them repeat by using a loop block. In this example, the loop block is set to "4." When Tracker repeats the actions four times, it ends up back where it started! This code includes a comment block, as well as start and stop blocks. You can now code Tracker to drive in a square.

Getting comfortable with Mindstorms programming language is easy because it's so fun to use! However, it's just the first step in the world of coding. There are many more programming languages out there for you to explore. Have fun coding!

Breaking the Code

Mindstorms is fun to use by yourself, but it can be even more fun when you share the coding process with friends. In the professional world, teams of programmers often work together on the same project. This helps save time. Each programmer does a small part of the code, and then they link their pieces together. A lot of planning and testing goes into the smaller parts before linking them together. This helps ensure that the pieces fit together correctly.

Before you begin programming, plan the actions you want your robot to complete. Document your program using the content window and comment blocks.

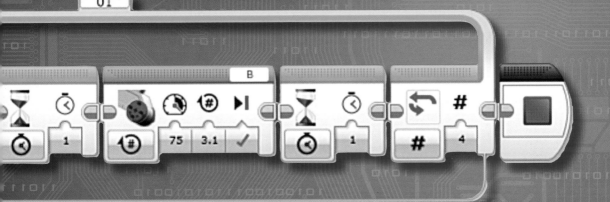

More Mindstorms Coding Blocks

medium motor - The medium motor is a smaller, lighter motor that turns faster than the large motor. It is often used to move parts of a robot, like grippers or hammers you build.

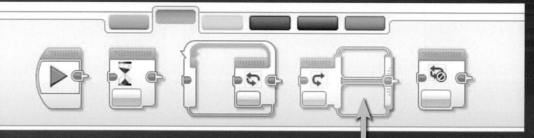

switch - The switch is used to test if input is true or false. It works a little like an IF statement in programs like Ruby, where code is written out.

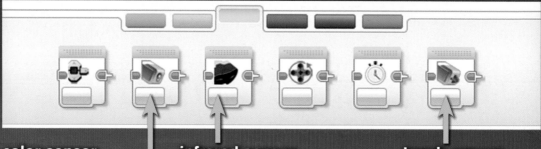

color sensor

Senses eight colors and can tell when intensity changes.

infrared sensor

Senses items close to the robot and reads signals sent by the transmitter.

touch sensor

Senses when it bumps something.

Glossary

engineer: Someone who plans and builds machines.

environment: The combination of computer hardware and software that allows a user to perform various tasks.

graphical: Having to do with graphics, or pictures and shapes.

hardware: The physical parts of a computer system, such as wires, hard drives, keyboards, and monitors.

iconic: Widely recognized and well liked.

infinity: An unlimited amount of time.

infrared: Light that people can't detect, but which can be seen by special technology.

interface: A system that allows two things, such as a person and a computer, to communicate with each other.

logic: A proper or reasonable way of thinking about or understanding something.

90-degree: Having to do with an angle that measures 90 degrees; also called a right angle.

pivot: To turn around a central point.

port: An opening in a computer by which it can be connected to another device using a special wire.

software: A program that runs on a computer and performs certain tasks.

USB connection: A connection formed between a computer and another device for the purpose of sharing data.

Index

Websites